ASOGWA JOY LOVE

Bridges to Tomorrow

Copyright © 2024 by Asogwa Joy Love

All rights reserved. No part of this publication may be reproduced, stored or transmitted in any form or by any means, electronic, mechanical, photocopying, recording, scanning, or otherwise without written permission from the publisher. It is illegal to copy this book, post it to a website, or distribute it by any other means without permission.

Asogwa Joy Love asserts the moral right to be identified as the author of this work.

Asogwa Joy Love has no responsibility for the persistence or accuracy of URLs for external or third-party Internet Websites referred to in this publication and does not guarantee that any content on such Websites is, or will remain, accurate or appropriate.

First edition

This book was professionally typeset on Reedsy.
Find out more at reedsy.com

Contents

1	The Chance Encounter	1
2	Whispers in the Shadows	5
3	Echoes of the Past	10
4	Under the Surface	15
5	The Dead Drop	19
6	In the Crosshairs	23
7	The Silent Witness	27
8	Shadows of Betrayal	33
9	Beneath the Surface	39
10	The Fractured Trust	45
11	Undercover Shadows	50
12	The Final Gambit	55

1

The Chance Encounter

Raindrops splattered against the window of the downtown café, a rhythmic patter that seemed to echo the pulsing anxiety of Mia Caldwell as she stared out at the gray, overcast sky. She was alone at a corner table, nursing a steaming cup of black coffee, the bitter aroma filling her senses as she tried to lose herself in the pages of a well-worn novel. The café was a quiet refuge from the chaos of her life, a place where she could temporarily escape from the whirlwind of deadlines and decisions that had been consuming her lately.

The door swung open with a creak, and the chime of the bell above it pulled Mia's gaze from her book. She glanced up, her eyes briefly meeting those of a newcomer. He was a tall man in his early thirties, dressed in a dark trench coat that contrasted sharply with the drab weather outside. His disheveled hair and unshaven face hinted at a life lived in turmoil, yet his eyes—sharp and intense—suggested a focus and determination that was almost palpable. He scanned the room with a quick, almost nervous glance before settling on the table opposite Mia's.

Mia quickly looked back at her book, pretending to be absorbed in the text as she felt the weight of his presence. There was something about him that intrigued her, though she couldn't quite place it. She tried to ignore the stirring curiosity and concentrated on her coffee. The minutes ticked by in silence, broken only by the soft clinking of cutlery and the occasional murmur of conversation from the other patrons.

Suddenly, there was a loud thud, followed by a soft gasp. Mia's head snapped up to see the man standing over his table, his face pale. He looked around frantically as if searching for something or someone. His eyes locked with hers for a split second before he hurriedly grabbed his coat and made a beeline for the door. The bell above the entrance chimed again as he rushed out into the rain.

Mia's heart raced. She felt a surge of adrenaline and a strange compulsion to follow him. Something was clearly wrong, and despite her better judgment, she found herself slipping out of her seat and heading toward the door. The café's warmth was immediately replaced by the cold, drizzling rain as she stepped outside, squinting through the misty veil to catch sight of the man.

He was already several yards ahead, moving with a determined stride, his coat flapping wildly in the wind. Mia hesitated for a moment, unsure of what to do. Her instincts pushed her forward, and she quickened her pace, her shoes splashing through puddles as she tried to keep up. She was almost close enough to call out to him when he ducked into a narrow alleyway between two old brick buildings.

With a deep breath, Mia entered the alley, her eyes adjusting to the dim light. The alley was cramped and littered with garbage, the smell of damp refuse filling the air. She could hear the man's hurried footsteps echoing off the walls as he continued to move deeper into the alley. Mia followed cautiously, her senses heightened and alert.

As she turned a corner, she caught sight of him again, now leaning against the wall, his breathing ragged. He was holding something tightly in his hands, but

Mia couldn't make out what it was from her vantage point. Her pulse quickened as she approached slowly, her footsteps muffled by the wet ground. Just as she was about to call out to him, a sudden, sharp noise made her freeze. It was the sound of a car engine revving up, growing louder and more menacing.

The man's head snapped up, his eyes wide with fear. He shoved the object he had been holding into his coat pocket and started moving toward the end of the alley. Mia's heart skipped a beat as she saw the shadowy figure of a car emerge from the end of the alley, its headlights cutting through the rain. The vehicle slowed, its engine growling as it approached.

Panic surged through Mia. She had no idea who was in the car or what was happening, but she knew she had to act. She called out to the man, her voice trembling with urgency. "Hey! Wait!"

The man glanced back, his eyes filled with a mix of desperation and caution. He took one last look at Mia before breaking into a sprint, his form disappearing into the darkness beyond the alley. The car screeched to a halt, and the driver's side door swung open. A tall figure in a dark suit stepped out, scanning the alley with a grim expression. Mia's breath caught in her throat as she realized she was now part of something she barely understood.

She backed away slowly, her mind racing. The figure in the suit noticed her and began to approach. Mia turned and fled, her heart pounding as she dashed back toward the café, rain pouring down her face. She burst through the door, slamming it behind her and leaning against it as she gasped for breath. The café was quiet once more, the normalcy of the environment starkly contrasting the chaos she had just left behind.

Mia's thoughts churned as she tried to make sense of what had happened. The man, the mysterious object, and the ominous car—it all felt like a puzzle with missing pieces. She looked around at the few remaining patrons, wondering if they had witnessed anything unusual. But no one seemed to have noticed her frantic entrance.

She took a shaky sip of her now-cold coffee, her mind racing. The chance encounter had left her with more questions than answers, and she couldn't shake the feeling that she had just stumbled into something far bigger than herself.

2

Whispers in the Shadows

The next morning, the sky was a thin, washed-out gray, and the drizzle from the previous night had left the city streets slick and reflective. Mia Caldwell awoke with a sense of unease, the events from the alleyway still vivid in her mind. She tried to shake off the discomfort as she prepared for her day, but a nagging curiosity about the man and the shadowy figure haunted her thoughts.

She made her way to her office, a small, bright space in a high-rise building downtown. As she sat at her desk, surrounded by stacks of paperwork and the hum of her computer, her mind kept wandering back to the alley. The man's fearful expression and the menacing car seemed to play on a loop in her head.

Mia shook her head, trying to focus on her work. She had just started typing an email when her phone buzzed. It was a text message from an unknown number:

"Meet me at the old warehouse on 4th Street. I have something important to tell you. Don't tell anyone."

Her pulse quickened. She looked around her office, half-expecting someone to be watching her. She quickly deleted the message, trying to calm the flutter of anxiety in her chest. Who could this be? And why were they contacting her? Her curiosity battled with her better judgment, but the nagging feeling that she needed to know more about what had happened the night before pushed her to make a decision.

By midday, the rain had stopped, leaving the city air heavy and damp. Mia decided to take a break and clear her head. She walked to a nearby park, where she found a bench and sat, the cool breeze brushing against her face. As she pondered her next move, her phone buzzed again, but this time it was a call from a familiar number: her friend and occasional confidant, Jenna.

"Mia, hey, I need to talk to you," Jenna said, her voice tight with concern. "I'm sorry to call you at work, but something strange happened."

"What's going on?" Mia asked, trying to mask her own unease.

"I got a message last night, too," Jenna said. "It was from an anonymous number, just like yours. It said something about meeting at the warehouse. I didn't think much of it, but it's really freaking me out."

Mia's heart skipped a beat. "That's exactly what I got. What did it say?"

"Just that it's important and not to tell anyone," Jenna replied. "I'm worried. I don't know what's going on, but I feel like we're being watched."

Mia glanced around the park, feeling a sudden chill. "I'm going to go. I think I need to find out what's happening."

Jenna hesitated. "Are you sure? It sounds risky."

"I don't know, Jenna. I have to know what's going on. I'll call you as soon as I can."

With a heavy sigh, Jenna agreed, and Mia ended the call. She headed back to her office to grab her things, her mind racing with thoughts of what awaited her at the warehouse. The old building on 4th Street was a place she had heard about but never visited—an abandoned structure with a reputation for being eerie and dangerous.

By late afternoon, Mia found herself standing in front of the dilapidated warehouse. The building loomed ahead, its metal facade rusted and covered in graffiti. The sky overhead was darker now, and the chill in the air hinted at the approaching evening. She hesitated for a moment, staring at the darkened entrance.

Taking a deep breath, she pushed open the creaking door and stepped inside. The warehouse was dimly lit by the weak sunlight filtering through broken windows. Dust motes danced in the air, and the scent of decay and mildew was thick. Her footsteps echoed as she moved deeper into the building, her phone clutched tightly in her hand.

"Hello?" she called, her voice trembling slightly. "Is anyone here?"

The only response was the hollow sound of her own voice reverberating through the empty space. She moved cautiously, her senses heightened, every creak and groan of the building making her jump.

As she rounded a corner, she spotted a shadowy figure standing at the far end of the warehouse. The figure was tall and cloaked in a dark coat, the same type the man from the alley had worn. Mia's heart raced as she took a step forward.

"Are you the one who sent the message?" she asked, trying to keep her voice steady.

The figure turned slowly, revealing a face she didn't recognize—a man with sharp features and cold, calculating eyes. He looked at her with a mixture of curiosity and disdain. "You're Mia Caldwell, aren't you?"

Mia nodded, her throat dry. "Yes. Who are you? What's this about?"

The man took a step closer, his gaze intense. "You don't understand the danger you're in. You saw something last night that was never meant for your eyes."

Mia swallowed hard. "What do you mean? I don't know what's going on."

The man's eyes narrowed. "You were a witness to something far more significant than you realize. The man you saw and the car that followed him—they're connected to something dangerous. You need to stay away from this."

Before Mia could respond, a loud bang echoed through the warehouse, and the sound of shuffling footsteps filled the air. The man's eyes widened in alarm. "We've been compromised," he said urgently. "You need to leave, now!"

Panic surged through Mia as she turned to run, her heart pounding. She raced toward the exit, her footsteps echoing in the empty space. The warehouse was a maze of shadows and debris, and she had to navigate through the clutter as she made her way back to the door.

Behind her, she could hear the sounds of pursuit—heavy footsteps and low voices. She burst through the door and out into the fading daylight, the cold air hitting her face. She glanced back and saw a group of figures emerging from the warehouse, their faces obscured by the shadows.

Mia sprinted to her car, fumbling with her keys as she unlocked the door. She jumped inside and slammed it shut, her breath coming in ragged gasps. As she sped away from the warehouse, she glanced in the rearview mirror, but the figures had disappeared.

Her mind raced with questions and fear. Who were those people, and why were they so intent on keeping her away from the warehouse? What was the danger she had stumbled into? As she drove away, she knew that whatever she had uncovered was only the beginning.

3

Echoes of the Past

The night settled heavily over the city, shrouding everything in a blanket of darkness. Mia Caldwell lay awake in her small apartment, staring at the ceiling. The events of the day replayed in her mind like a relentless film. She couldn't shake the image of the shadowy figures emerging from the warehouse or the chilling encounter with the mysterious man. Her phone buzzed on the nightstand, breaking the silence. The text message was from Jenna:

"Any news? I'm worried about you."

Mia's fingers hovered over the screen as she typed a quick reply:

"I'm fine, just need some time to think. I'll call you tomorrow."

She set her phone aside, trying to calm her racing thoughts. The feeling of being watched, of danger lurking around every corner, was almost too much to bear. Exhaustion finally claimed her, and she drifted into an uneasy sleep.

The next morning, the first light of dawn filtered through the blinds, casting a pale glow over the room. Mia awoke to a persistent ringing sound. She groggily reached for her phone, expecting a call from work, but was startled to see a number she didn't recognize. She answered cautiously.

"Mia Caldwell?" a gruff voice asked.

"Yes, this is she," Mia replied, her heart skipping a beat.

"This is Detective Harris from the local precinct. I need you to come down to the station. We have some questions about the incident at the warehouse last night."

Mia's blood ran cold. "I don't understand. What incident?"

"Just come in, please. It's important."

The line went dead before she could respond. She stared at her phone, the words of the detective echoing in her mind. What had happened at the warehouse that warranted police involvement? She quickly dressed and made her way to the precinct, her mind a whirlwind of possibilities.

The precinct was bustling with activity when Mia arrived, and she was ushered into a small interrogation room. Detective Harris, a tall man with a stern expression and dark circles under his eyes, sat at the table, his gaze steady and unyielding.

"Have a seat," he said, gesturing to a chair across from him.

Mia sat down, trying to remain calm. "I'm here. What's this about?"

Detective Harris folded his arms. "We received a report of suspicious activity at the warehouse on 4th Street last night. Witnesses said they saw someone leaving the scene in a hurry. Given your presence there, we need to know what you saw."

Mia's throat went dry. "I—I saw a man in a dark coat. He was nervous, and then he left quickly. I followed him because I was concerned, and then I saw a car pulling up. That's when things got really tense, and I had to leave."

The detective's gaze was intense. "And what about the other people you saw? Did you recognize them?"

Mia shook her head. "No, I didn't get a good look at them. They were in the shadows."

Detective Harris leaned forward. "We've been investigating that warehouse for a while now. It's been linked to several criminal activities, but we haven't been able to get concrete evidence. Your sighting might be crucial. Can you remember anything else?"

Mia racked her brain, but the details were elusive. "I—I don't know. It was all so sudden and chaotic."

The detective's eyes narrowed. "If you remember anything, anything at all, let us know. This is serious, Mia."

With that, Detective Harris dismissed her, and Mia left the precinct feeling unsettled. As she walked to her car, her phone buzzed again, this time with a message from Jenna:

"I'm outside your apartment. Can we talk?"

Mia sighed and drove back home, her thoughts swirling. When she arrived, Jenna was waiting by the door, her face pale and anxious.

"Hey," Mia said, trying to sound casual.

Jenna looked at her with concern. "What did the detective want? Are you okay?"

Mia unlocked the door and led Jenna inside. "I'm not sure. They were just asking questions about the warehouse. They said it's connected to some criminal activities."

Jenna's eyes widened. "That's serious. What did you see?"

Mia recounted the events as best as she could, watching Jenna's expression shift from concern to fear. "I don't know why they're so interested in me. I was just there by accident."

Jenna shook her head. "I don't think it's a coincidence. You saw something important, and now they're worried."

Mia nodded, feeling the weight of Jenna's words. "I think we need to figure out what's really going on. There's something bigger here, and I don't want to be in the dark about it."

Jenna agreed. "I'll help you, but we need to be careful. If those people are involved, they might come after us too."

The two friends spent the rest of the day researching the warehouse and its history. They discovered that it had been a site of various criminal activities over the years, including drug trafficking and illegal arms deals. The more they uncovered, the more they realized how dangerous their situation had become.

As night fell, Mia and Jenna made a plan. They decided to return to the warehouse, this time with a more cautious approach. They wanted to find out if there was any concrete evidence of the criminal activities and, hopefully, shed light on why they had been dragged into this.

Before leaving, Jenna pulled out a small flashlight and handed it to Mia. "We need to be prepared. This might get dangerous."

Mia took the flashlight, her nerves on edge. "Let's hope we can find something useful without getting ourselves into trouble."

With their resolve set, they headed back to the warehouse. The darkness seemed even more oppressive than before, and every sound was magnified in the silence. They approached the building cautiously, the shadows stretching and shifting in the dim light.

As they entered, Mia felt a shiver of fear. The warehouse was eerily quiet, the only sound the echo of their footsteps. They moved through the space, their flashlights cutting through the darkness as they searched for clues.

Mia couldn't shake the feeling that they were being watched. Every creak and groan of the building seemed to amplify her anxiety. The tension was palpable, and the air felt thick with unspoken threats.

Suddenly, Jenna stopped and pointed to a small, hidden alcove near the back of the warehouse. "Look," she whispered.

In the dim light, Mia could make out a metal box partially hidden behind some crates. Her heart raced as she approached it, her hands trembling. She opened the box, and inside, she found a collection of documents and photographs—evidence that hinted at the warehouse's involvement in illegal activities.

Mia and Jenna exchanged a look of determination. They had uncovered something significant, but they also knew they were now in deeper than ever. The echoes of the past were coming back to haunt them, and the danger was far from over.

4

Under the Surface

The warehouse loomed ominously in the darkness as Mia and Jenna made their way back to their apartment, their minds racing with the implications of their discovery. The documents they had found were a trove of evidence detailing illicit transactions and connections to organized crime. They had managed to snap a few photos of the documents with Jenna's phone, but they knew they had to tread carefully.

As they arrived at Mia's apartment, they locked the door behind them and settled at the kitchen table, the tension in the room almost palpable. The flickering light from the overhead lamp cast long shadows across the walls.

"I can't believe what we found," Jenna said, her voice trembling. "This is huge."

Mia nodded, her thoughts racing. "We need to figure out what to do with this information. If we go to the police, we might be putting ourselves in even more danger."

Jenna looked at her with wide eyes. "But if we don't go to the authorities, we're just sitting on evidence that could be critical."

Mia ran a hand through her hair, feeling the weight of the decision pressing down on her. "Let's review what we have first. Maybe there's something in these documents that can guide us on the best course of action."

They spread the photos out on the table, examining the documents closely. There were financial records, lists of names, and photographs of various locations. One photograph in particular caught Mia's attention—it was a picture of a man, one she recognized from the warehouse. He was standing next to a nondescript building, its address scrawled in the corner.

"This building," Mia said, pointing to the photograph. "I've seen it before. It's not far from here, just on the edge of the industrial district."

Jenna squinted at the photo. "Are you sure? It might be worth checking out."

Mia nodded, her mind made up. "Let's go take a look. Maybe there's something there that can give us more context about these documents."

They left the apartment, the night air cool and crisp against their faces. The drive to the industrial district was silent, each of them lost in their thoughts. The city lights flickered past as they navigated the labyrinthine streets until they arrived at the building from the photograph.

The building was an old warehouse, much like the one they had visited before, but it looked more well-maintained. There were no signs of recent activity, and the area around it was eerily quiet. Mia parked the car a few blocks away, and they approached the building on foot, their footsteps echoing in the still night.

They circled the building, looking for an entrance. The back door was partially ajar, and they slipped inside, their flashlights cutting through the darkness.

The interior was dusty and cluttered, with old machinery and stacks of crates piled haphazardly. The faint sound of dripping water added to the eerie atmosphere.

As they explored, Mia and Jenna moved cautiously, their senses on high alert. They turned a corner and found themselves in what looked like an office space, though it was barely functional. An old desk sat in the center of the room, covered in grime and cobwebs. On the desk was a folder, its contents partially visible. Mia's heart raced as she approached and opened it, revealing more documents similar to the ones they had found earlier, but with additional details.

"This could be a significant lead," Mia whispered, flipping through the papers. "It looks like there's a list of meetings and contact information for key players."

Jenna leaned in to examine the papers. "This could help us understand who's involved and maybe even why they're interested in us."

Suddenly, a noise from the hallway made them both freeze. The sound of footsteps—slow and deliberate—echoed through the building. Mia's breath caught in her throat as she glanced at Jenna, her eyes wide with fear.

"We need to hide," Mia whispered urgently.

They scrambled to find cover, hiding behind a stack of crates. The footsteps grew louder, and the door to the office creaked open. A figure stepped inside, their silhouette dark and menacing. Mia could barely make out the shape of a man, dressed in a dark coat and hat, much like the one she had seen at the warehouse.

The man began to rummage through the desk, his movements quick and agitated. Mia and Jenna held their breath, trying to remain as silent as possible.

Mia's heart pounded in her chest as she watched the man's actions.

After a few tense minutes, the man straightened up and turned to leave, clutching a briefcase tightly. He paused at the door, glancing back into the room as if sensing that something was amiss. Mia and Jenna barely breathed, their bodies tensed and ready to move.

The man eventually left, closing the door behind him. Mia and Jenna waited for what felt like an eternity before emerging from their hiding spot. The tension in the room was palpable as they assessed the situation.

"That was close," Jenna said, her voice shaky. "We need to get out of here before he comes back."

Mia nodded in agreement. They quickly gathered the documents and made their way back to the car, their hearts still racing. The drive back to the apartment was fraught with anxiety, their minds racing with thoughts of what they had seen and what it meant for their safety.

When they finally reached Mia's apartment, they took a moment to catch their breath. The documents were spread out on the kitchen table once again, and the weight of their discovery settled heavily on them.

"We have more pieces of the puzzle," Mia said, her voice determined. "But we need to be careful. We're in deeper than we thought."

Jenna nodded, her expression resolute. "We'll figure this out. We just need to stay focused and keep each other safe."

As they continued to examine the documents, the reality of their situation began to sink in. The shadows of their past encounters were closing in, and the danger was far from over.

5

The Dead Drop

The following morning, the city was cloaked in a dense fog that clung to the buildings like a shroud. Mia and Jenna had barely slept, their minds still reeling from the close encounter at the warehouse. They had spent hours reviewing the documents they'd found, but the more they read, the more questions arose. What were the connections between the names and locations? And who were the people behind the shadows they had seen?

At dawn, Mia drove Jenna to her apartment, and they agreed to meet later to continue their investigation. Mia's thoughts were a tangled mess of anxiety and determination. She had decided to visit the address from the photograph, a nondescript building on the edge of town, hoping to find additional clues.

As she arrived at the building, the fog had begun to lift, but the air remained heavy and oppressive. The building was a gray, utilitarian structure with no distinguishing features. It looked abandoned, but Mia knew better. She parked a few blocks away and approached on foot, her senses alert for any sign of activity.

She circled the building, searching for any sign of entry. In the back, she discovered a small door partially obscured by overgrown weeds. She pulled out her flashlight and tested the door—it was unlocked. Her heart pounded as she pushed it open, revealing a dimly lit corridor.

Mia entered cautiously, her footsteps echoing softly in the empty space. The corridor led to a series of rooms, all of which appeared to be in disrepair. Dust and cobwebs filled the corners, and the smell of mildew was strong. She continued down the hall, her flashlight beam cutting through the darkness.

In one of the rooms, Mia noticed a metal filing cabinet partially hidden behind a stack of old crates. Her pulse quickened as she approached it. The cabinet was locked, but she found a set of old tools on a nearby workbench. She tried to pick the lock, her hands trembling with both fear and excitement.

After several minutes of fumbling with the lock, it clicked open. Inside, she found a collection of files and folders, all meticulously labeled. Her fingers shook as she flipped through them. There were more documents detailing transactions, meeting notes, and photographs of various individuals.

One photograph caught her eye—a close-up of a man she had seen at the warehouse. The photo was marked with a red X, and next to it was a handwritten note that read: "Eliminate before the drop."

Mia's heart raced as she realized the implication. The term "dead drop" was familiar to her from her research into criminal networks. It referred to a covert method of exchanging information or goods. The note suggested that the man was a target, and the "drop" was an imminent event.

Her phone buzzed with a text from Jenna:

"Are you okay? I'm getting worried. Call me when you can."

Mia quickly replied, trying to keep her voice steady:

"I'm at the building from the photo. Found more documents. Will call soon."

As she continued to examine the files, a noise from the corridor made her freeze. Footsteps, deliberate and heavy, approached. Mia's heart raced as she hurried to close the cabinet and hide behind the crates. She held her breath, straining to hear.

The footsteps grew louder and closer. Mia could see the shadow of a figure moving past the doorway. She waited, barely daring to breathe. The figure paused at the door, and Mia heard the sound of a key turning in the lock. The door creaked open, and the figure stepped inside.

Mia's mind raced as she tried to make out the figure's features in the dim light. The person moved deliberately, searching through the room. Mia's pulse pounded in her ears as she remained hidden, her fingers gripping her flashlight tightly.

The figure seemed to be methodically checking every corner of the room. After what felt like an eternity, the figure turned and walked back toward the door. Mia waited until the door clicked shut and the footsteps faded away before she dared to move.

She quickly gathered the files, her hands shaking with urgency. She knew she had to get out of there before the figure returned. As she exited the building, she glanced around, her eyes scanning for any signs of danger. The fog had begun to lift, revealing the clear morning sky, but the air still felt heavy with unspoken threats.

Mia drove to Jenna's apartment, her mind racing with the implications of what she had discovered. The "dead drop" reference suggested that something significant was about to happen, and the man marked for elimination was in immediate danger.

When she arrived, Jenna opened the door with a worried expression. "What happened? Are you alright?"

Mia quickly recounted her findings and the encounter at the building. Jenna listened intently, her face growing increasingly concerned. "This is bigger than we thought," Jenna said. "We need to figure out what the dead drop is and if we can stop it."

Mia nodded, her resolve hardening. "We need to act fast. The documents suggest that there might be a scheduled exchange or meeting. If we can find out where and when, we might be able to prevent whatever is about to happen."

They pored over the documents, searching for any clues about the location and timing of the dead drop. The documents were filled with cryptic notes and references to locations Mia and Jenna didn't recognize. But one entry stood out: a series of coordinates and a time.

"This looks like a location," Jenna said, pointing to the coordinates. "If we can pinpoint this, we might find out where the dead drop is scheduled to occur."

Mia nodded, feeling a surge of determination. "Let's figure out these coordinates and see if we can get there before it's too late."

As they worked, the sense of urgency grew. The stakes were higher than ever, and the danger was closing in. They knew they had to act quickly to uncover the truth and prevent a potential disaster. The shadows of their investigation were growing darker, and the path ahead was fraught with uncertainty.

6

In the Crosshairs

The coordinates from the documents led Mia and Jenna to an isolated industrial area on the outskirts of the city, far from the bustling core they were used to. It was late afternoon, and the sun hung low in the sky, casting long shadows across the desolate streets. The air was thick with tension as they approached the coordinates, both women aware of the gravity of their situation.

Mia drove slowly through the area, her eyes scanning the buildings for any sign of activity. The streets were eerily quiet, lined with abandoned factories and warehouses. They finally arrived at an old, rusting building that matched the coordinates—a decrepit structure with broken windows and a sagging roof.

"I think this is it," Jenna said, her voice barely more than a whisper. "It looks like the right place."

Mia nodded, her grip tightening on the steering wheel. "Let's park a bit further away and approach on foot. We don't want to attract any attention."

They parked a few blocks away and walked cautiously toward the building. The sense of danger was palpable, and every sound seemed amplified in the quiet. They approached the building's back entrance, a heavy metal door partially ajar. Mia nudged it open and they slipped inside, their flashlights cutting through the darkness.

The interior of the building was as dilapidated as the outside—dust-covered machinery and broken pallets scattered across the floor. The air was thick with the smell of rust and decay. They moved quietly, their footsteps muffled by the layers of grime on the floor.

Mia and Jenna made their way deeper into the building, their flashlights revealing a maze of corridors and storage rooms. The feeling of being watched was intense, and every creak of the building seemed to amplify their anxiety. They followed the layout suggested by the documents, heading toward a large, open space at the heart of the building.

As they approached, they noticed a faint sound—voices. They stopped in their tracks, listening intently. The voices were low and indistinct, but they were definitely coming from somewhere nearby. Mia and Jenna exchanged worried glances and moved cautiously toward the source of the sound.

The voices led them to a large, open room with high ceilings and a few remaining support columns. From their vantage point, they could see a group of men gathered around a makeshift table in the center of the room. The men were dressed in dark clothing and appeared to be engaged in a heated discussion.

Mia's heart raced as she recognized one of the men from the photographs they had found—the same man with the red X. He was talking animatedly, gesturing with his hands. The other men listened intently, their faces grim and serious.

"Those must be the people behind the dead drop," Jenna whispered. "We need to figure out what they're planning."

Mia nodded, her eyes fixed on the group. She tried to make out the details of their conversation, but the distance and the muffled tones made it difficult. She noticed a large, black briefcase on the table, similar to the one the man from the warehouse had carried.

Just then, one of the men glanced toward the entrance, his eyes narrowing. Mia and Jenna quickly ducked behind a stack of crates, their hearts pounding. The man's gaze lingered on their hiding spot, and for a moment, Mia feared they had been spotted. But the man turned away, and the conversation continued.

They waited, barely breathing, as the discussion seemed to reach a climax. The men began to disperse, heading toward various exits. Mia's pulse quickened as she realized they were about to leave. She signaled to Jenna, and they carefully moved toward the table.

The briefcase was still there, and Mia approached it cautiously. She opened it, her breath catching in her throat. Inside were stacks of cash, documents, and several small packages wrapped in brown paper. The sight confirmed her worst fears—this was a major exchange, likely involving illegal transactions.

"We need to get this to the authorities," Jenna said, her voice trembling. "This could be the evidence we need to stop them."

Mia nodded in agreement, but they both knew they had to be careful. They gathered the documents and a few of the packages, ensuring they had as much evidence as possible. Just as they were about to leave, the sound of a door slamming shut echoed through the building.

Panic surged through Mia and Jenna as they realized they might be trapped. They hurried to the exit, but the door they had used to enter was now firmly closed. The men were coming back, their voices growing louder. Mia's mind raced as she searched for another way out.

They moved through the building, their flashlights casting eerie shadows on the walls. The sound of footsteps grew closer, and Mia could feel the pressure mounting. They found a small window near the floor and managed to force it open. It was a tight squeeze, but they had no other choice.

"Go first," Mia urged Jenna. "I'll follow right after."

Jenna squeezed through the window and landed outside, her hands gripping the edge as she helped Mia out. The building was now a dark silhouette against the fading light of the day. They quickly made their way back to the car, their nerves frayed and their hearts pounding.

As they drove away, Mia glanced in the rearview mirror, but there were no signs of pursuit. The danger was not yet over, but they had taken a significant step in uncovering the truth. The evidence they had gathered was crucial, and they knew they had to get it to the authorities as soon as possible.

When they arrived back at Jenna's apartment, they reviewed the documents and packages one more time, ensuring everything was in order. The evidence was compelling, and Mia was determined to see it through to the end. They prepared a detailed report and contacted the authorities, their resolve unwavering despite the fear that still gripped them.

As night fell, Mia and Jenna sat in silence, the weight of their discovery heavy on their shoulders. They knew the risks they were facing, but their commitment to uncovering the truth and bringing those responsible to justice drove them forward. The path ahead was fraught with danger, but they were ready to face it head-on, determined to make a difference and stop the dark forces threatening their city.

7

The Silent Witness

The early morning sun barely penetrated the heavy curtains of Jenna's apartment, casting a dim glow across the room. Mia and Jenna sat at the kitchen table, the evidence from the previous night spread out before them. The atmosphere was tense, punctuated only by the soft hum of Jenna's coffee maker.

Mia sifted through the documents, her mind racing with the implications of what they had uncovered. The men they had seen were clearly involved in a complex network of criminal activity. The cash and packages they had discovered pointed to a significant operation, but they needed to connect the dots to fully understand what was happening.

Jenna paced nervously, her phone clutched in her hand. "I'm really starting to worry," she said, her voice tight with anxiety. "We haven't heard from the authorities yet. What if they don't take us seriously?"

Mia looked up from the documents, her expression resolute. "We've done everything we can to provide them with solid evidence. It's up to them now. But we need to stay vigilant. If these people are as dangerous as we think, they might come after us."

Jenna nodded, her worry evident. "You're right. We need to be careful."

They spent the morning organizing their findings and preparing to meet with the authorities. As they worked, Mia's phone buzzed with a new message. It was from Detective Harris.

"We need to talk. Meet me at the precinct."

Mia exchanged a worried glance with Jenna. "This might be the breakthrough we've been waiting for."

They arrived at the precinct just before noon, their nerves on edge. Detective Harris met them in the lobby, his face grim. He led them to an interrogation room, where they began to review the evidence they had collected.

"I've gone through the documents and the photos you sent," Harris said, his tone serious. "This is significant. We're setting up a sting operation, but we need more information about the operation's details and participants."

Mia's heart sank. "We already provided everything we know. What else do you need?"

Harris sighed. "The information you've given us is helpful, but we need to be sure about who's involved and their connections. We also need to know if there's an imminent threat."

Mia felt a pang of frustration. "We saw the briefcase filled with cash and the packages. We know there's a major operation happening. Can't you act on that?"

Harris looked at her with a pained expression. "We're working on it. But we need concrete proof and confirmation before we move forward. We can't risk tipping them off."

Jenna's eyes flashed with anger. "So what do we do in the meantime? Just wait around while they potentially cover their tracks?"

Harris held up his hands. "I understand your frustration, but this is a delicate situation. We're coordinating with other departments to monitor the location and the suspects. In the meantime, I suggest you stay low and avoid drawing attention."

Mia and Jenna left the precinct feeling unsettled. They decided to head back to Jenna's apartment to regroup and strategize. The urgency of their situation was palpable, and they couldn't shake the feeling that time was running out.

As they drove, Mia's mind raced. She was convinced they were on the brink of uncovering something major, but they needed more than just the fragments they had. They needed to find out more about the "dead drop" and the individuals involved.

When they arrived back at Jenna's apartment, they decided to review the evidence one more time, looking for any overlooked details. As they pored over the documents, Jenna's phone rang. It was an unknown number.

Jenna answered hesitantly. "Hello?"

A voice on the other end was low and cautious. "Miss Caldwell? This is George from the tech department. I have something you might want to hear."

Mia's ears perked up as Jenna listened intently. "What is it?"

"Earlier today, we intercepted a communication from one of the suspects," George explained. "It mentioned a 'meeting point' and a specific time. I thought it might be related to the dead drop."

Mia's heart skipped a beat. "Can you send us the details?"

George agreed and sent over a message with coordinates and a time. Mia and Jenna examined the information, their eyes widening as they realized the location was not far from where they had been.

"This could be it," Jenna said, her voice tinged with excitement. "We need to get there before the meeting takes place."

They quickly gathered their things and set out, following the coordinates provided. The location was an abandoned office building in a more secluded part of town. The area was quiet, and the building appeared to be in a similar state of disrepair as the others they had seen.

They parked a safe distance away and approached the building cautiously. The sun was beginning to set, and the fading light cast long shadows across the desolate streets. They entered the building, their flashlights illuminating the dark, empty corridors.

As they moved through the building, they heard the faint sound of voices again. They followed the sound to a large, open room at the center of the building. The room was dimly lit by a single hanging lightbulb, casting eerie shadows across the floor.

Mia and Jenna positioned themselves behind a stack of crates, their breaths shallow and controlled. They could see several figures gathered in the center of the room, their voices low and urgent. One of the figures was the same man Mia had seen before, the one marked for elimination.

The conversation was heated, and Mia strained to hear the details. The man was discussing the distribution of the cash and packages they had seen before.

It became clear that this was a major transaction involving multiple parties.

Mia's heart pounded as she realized the gravity of the situation. They were on the verge of witnessing a major illegal operation, and the information they had gathered could be crucial in bringing the perpetrators to justice.

Suddenly, one of the figures glanced toward their hiding spot, and Mia's blood ran cold. She held her breath, her eyes locked on the figure. For a moment, it seemed as if they had been discovered.

But the figure turned away, and the conversation continued. Mia and Jenna remained hidden, their bodies tense with fear and anticipation. They knew they had to gather as much information as possible without being caught.

As the meeting progressed, the figures exchanged documents and briefcases, confirming the details of the transaction. Mia and Jenna watched in silence, knowing that their next move would be critical in ensuring that justice was served.

When the meeting finally concluded, the figures began to disperse. Mia and Jenna waited until the room was empty before emerging from their hiding spot. The evidence they had gathered was substantial, and they knew they had to act quickly.

As they left the building, the night air was cool and crisp, a stark contrast to the tense atmosphere inside. They made their way back to Jenna's apartment, their minds racing with the implications of what they had witnessed.

The next steps were clear: they needed to get the evidence to the authorities and ensure that the operation was shut down. The danger was far from over, but Mia and Jenna were determined to see it through to the end. The shadows of their investigation were growing darker, and they knew they had to stay vigilant to uncover the truth and stop the criminal network threatening their city.

8

Shadows of Betrayal

The city was draped in a heavy blanket of darkness as Mia and Jenna returned to their apartment after the tense meeting at the abandoned office building. They were exhausted, both physically and emotionally, but the urgency of their situation kept them alert. The evidence they had gathered was crucial, and they needed to ensure it reached the authorities without delay.

As they entered Jenna's apartment, Mia's phone buzzed with a new message. It was from Detective Harris.

"Need to see you ASAP. Urgent. Meet me at the precinct."

Mia's heart skipped a beat. "It looks like Harris wants to meet us immediately. This could be a breakthrough."

Jenna nodded, her expression tense. "Let's get moving."

They drove to the precinct in near silence, their thoughts consumed by the implications of their findings. The streets were eerily quiet, and the city lights seemed to flicker with an unsettling rhythm. When they arrived, Detective

Harris was waiting for them in the lobby, his face grave.

"Follow me," Harris said, leading them to a secure conference room. The room was sparsely furnished with a large table and a few chairs. On the table lay several documents and photographs, their significance unclear.

"Thank you for coming so quickly," Harris said as he closed the door behind them. "We've been analyzing the evidence you provided. It's clear that this operation is far-reaching and dangerous."

Mia and Jenna exchanged anxious glances. "What have you discovered?" Mia asked, her voice tight.

Harris leaned over the table and pointed to a series of documents. "These documents corroborate the information you found. They detail several key players and their roles in the operation. We've also identified the location where the next major transaction is supposed to take place."

Mia's pulse quickened. "Where is it?"

Harris tapped a map on the table. "It's an old warehouse on the outskirts of the city. We're planning a sting operation to intercept the transaction. But there's a catch."

Jenna frowned. "What's the catch?"

"There's been a security breach," Harris said, his expression darkening. "We have reason to believe that someone within our department might be compromised. We're taking extra precautions, but we need to be discreet. We don't want to tip off the suspects or the potential mole."

Mia's stomach churned with anxiety. "So what do you need from us?"

"We need you to be our eyes and ears," Harris explained. "You're already familiar with the layout and the players involved. We need you to keep an eye on the warehouse and provide real-time updates."

Mia nodded, her determination unwavering. "We'll do it."

Harris handed them a set of instructions and a walkie-talkie for communication. "Be careful. This is a high-risk operation, and we don't want to take any chances."

As they left the precinct, the weight of their task hung heavy on their shoulders. The warehouse was not far from where they had been previously, and they knew it would be a race against time to ensure the sting operation was successful.

They arrived at the warehouse just before midnight. The building was situated in a remote area, surrounded by tall fences and overgrown vegetation. The only sounds were the distant hum of traffic and the occasional rustle of leaves in the wind.

Mia and Jenna parked their car a safe distance away and approached the warehouse on foot. They found a vantage point from which they could observe the entrance without being seen. The moonlight cast long shadows across the ground, adding to the eerie atmosphere.

"Are you ready?" Jenna asked, her voice barely a whisper.

Mia nodded. "Let's do this."

They settled into their positions, their eyes trained on the warehouse entrance. The minutes ticked by slowly, each second stretching into an eternity. Mia's nerves were on edge as she scanned the area for any signs of movement.

Suddenly, headlights pierced the darkness as several vehicles approached the warehouse. Mia's heart raced as she recognized some of the figures from the previous meetings. The operation was beginning, and they needed to be ready.

The vehicles parked outside, and the figures began to unload boxes and briefcases. Mia and Jenna kept their distance, observing through binoculars. The warehouse door creaked open, and the figures disappeared inside.

Mia adjusted the walkie-talkie. "Detective Harris, this is Mia. The operation is underway. The suspects are inside the warehouse."

"Copy that," Harris's voice crackled through the speaker. "We're in position. Keep us updated."

Mia and Jenna watched as the suspects carried out their activities, their movements deliberate and methodical. The tension in the air was palpable as they observed the exchange of cash and documents.

As the minutes passed, Mia noticed something unusual. One of the figures, who had been relatively quiet, seemed to be communicating with someone on a phone. The conversation was brief but intense. Mia's instincts told her that this was important.

"Detective Harris, we have a situation," Mia said into the walkie-talkie. "One of the figures is on the phone. It looks like they're discussing something urgent."

"Stay alert," Harris instructed. "We're preparing to move in."

Mia's eyes remained locked on the figure. The conversation ended, and the person hurried toward a side exit. Mia's heart pounded as she realized that this could be a pivotal moment in the operation.

"Jenna, follow that figure," Mia whispered. "I'll stay here and keep watch."

Jenna nodded and carefully made her way toward the side exit, blending into the shadows. Mia watched as the figure disappeared around the corner of the building. Her mind raced with questions—who was this person meeting, and what were they planning?

The tension in the warehouse mounted as the suspects continued their transaction. Mia's gaze remained fixed on the entrance, waiting for the moment when the authorities would make their move. The wait seemed endless, and every creak of the building sent a jolt of anxiety through her.

Suddenly, the sound of sirens cut through the night. The warehouse was illuminated by flashing lights as police vehicles surrounded the building. Mia's heart raced with a mixture of relief and apprehension. The sting operation was underway.

From her vantage point, Mia could see the figures inside the warehouse scrambling. The authorities moved in swiftly, apprehending the suspects and seizing the evidence. Mia's phone buzzed with a message from Harris.

"Operation is successful. Good work. We'll need a detailed report from you."

Mia's mind was still reeling as she watched the scene unfold. Jenna returned, her expression tense but relieved.

"They were trying to make a deal with someone outside," Jenna said, her voice low. "But I couldn't see who it was."

Mia nodded, her thoughts already turning to the next steps. The operation had been a success, but the implications of what they had uncovered were still unfolding. The suspects were in custody, but the network they were part of was likely still active.

As they made their way back to the car, Mia and Jenna knew that their work was far from over. The shadows of betrayal and deception were deepening, and they were determined to see the investigation through to its conclusion. The truth was within reach, and they would stop at nothing to uncover it and bring those responsible to justice.

9

Beneath the Surface

The night was unusually still, the kind of quiet that made even the smallest noises seem louder. Mia and Jenna, exhausted but still on high alert, returned to Jenna's apartment after the successful sting operation. The city lights outside glimmered like distant stars, and the adrenaline from the previous events still pulsed through their veins. They needed to debrief and figure out their next move.

Inside Jenna's dimly lit apartment, the atmosphere was tense. The living room, strewn with evidence and scattered papers, was now a chaotic mix of documents and photographs. Mia and Jenna took a moment to collect their thoughts, the weight of their findings bearing down heavily on them.

Mia opened her laptop and began organizing the evidence they had collected. The documents from the warehouse operation, the intercepted communication, and the photographs of the suspects were all laid out in a meticulous order. She hoped that amidst the chaos, there would be something that could tie together the threads of their investigation.

Jenna poured two cups of coffee, her hands trembling slightly. She placed one in front of Mia and sat down across from her, her eyes focused on the scattered papers. "We need to go over everything again. Make sure we haven't missed anything."

Mia nodded, sipping the coffee and feeling the warmth spread through her. "Agreed. We need to ensure that everything is accounted for. There might be something crucial that we overlooked."

As they worked through the documents, Mia's phone buzzed with a new message. It was from Detective Harris.

"Need to meet. Urgent. Secure location. Details to follow."

Mia's heart raced as she read the message. "Harris wants to meet us again. It's urgent."

Jenna's expression shifted from worried to alert. "This doesn't sound good. Do you think something went wrong with the operation?"

Mia shook her head, her mind racing. "I don't know, but we need to find out. Let's get ready."

The message from Harris provided them with a new location—a small, inconspicuous office on the edge of town. As they drove through the darkened streets, the tension between them was palpable. The city seemed to be holding its breath, the quiet night amplifying their anxiety.

When they arrived at the location, they found the office building to be a nondescript structure, its windows dark and its exterior unremarkable. They entered the building and took the elevator to the third floor, following Harris's instructions. The hallway was empty, and the air was thick with anticipation.

Harris was waiting for them in a small, windowless conference room. The space was bare, with a single table and a few chairs. His face was a mask of concern, and he gestured for them to sit.

"Thank you for coming on such short notice," Harris said, his tone serious. "We have a problem."

Mia and Jenna exchanged worried glances. "What's happened?" Mia asked.

Harris took a deep breath. "After the sting operation, we conducted a preliminary review of the evidence. Everything seemed to be going smoothly until a few hours ago. We received a tip-off from an anonymous source claiming that there's a mole within our department. The tip included specific details about the operation that only someone inside would know."

Mia's heart sank. "So the mole could have jeopardized the operation?"

Harris nodded gravely. "Exactly. We need to figure out who the mole is and what they've shared. We also need to ensure the safety of everyone involved. The stakes have just gotten higher."

Jenna's face was pale with concern. "What do we do now?"

"We need to be cautious," Harris said. "We're conducting an internal investigation to identify the mole. In the meantime, I need you both to stay alert and avoid any unnecessary contact. The suspects we arrested might have allies who could be looking for retribution."

Mia's mind raced with the implications. "What about the evidence we collected? Shouldn't we secure it?"

Harris nodded. "Yes. I've arranged for a secure facility to store the evidence. I'll have it picked up and transported immediately. But we need to ensure that we don't draw attention to ourselves."

As Harris made the necessary arrangements, Mia and Jenna waited in tense silence. The weight of their situation was pressing down on them, and the sense of urgency was overwhelming. The thought of a mole within the department made their mission even more perilous.

After a few tense moments, Harris returned with an update. "The evidence is on its way to the secure facility. I'll keep you informed about the internal investigation. In the meantime, we need to stay low and avoid any contact with the suspects or their associates."

Mia and Jenna left the office, their minds reeling with the new developments. They knew they had to be careful, but the uncertainty of the situation made every decision feel crucial. As they drove back to Jenna's apartment, the city's familiar landmarks seemed foreign, their sense of security shattered.

Back at Jenna's apartment, they tried to regain their composure. The documents and photographs lay scattered on the table, their significance heightened by the new threat they faced. They decided to review everything once more, hoping to uncover any overlooked details.

As they worked, Jenna's phone rang. The caller ID showed an unknown number. Jenna hesitated before answering.

"Hello?"

A distorted voice on the other end spoke quickly. "You don't know me, but I have information about the operation and the mole. Meet me at the old docks in an hour. Come alone."

The line went dead before Jenna could respond. She turned to Mia, her face pale. "That was unsettling. What do you think?"

Mia's expression was grim. "It could be a trap, or it could be genuine. Either way, we need to find out what they know."

They prepared for the meeting, their nerves on edge. The docks were a secluded area, and the thought of meeting an unknown informant there was nerve-wracking. They drove to the location in silence, the tension between them palpable.

The docks were deserted, the only sounds the distant murmur of the city and the occasional creak of old wooden planks. They parked the car and approached the meeting spot, a dimly lit area near a large shipping container.

Mia's heart pounded as they waited, their eyes scanning the shadows for any signs of movement. The minutes ticked by slowly, each second stretching into an eternity. The sense of danger was overwhelming, and the silence seemed to press in on them.

Suddenly, a figure emerged from the shadows, their face obscured by a hood. The figure approached cautiously, their movements deliberate.

"Are you the ones who received the message?" the figure asked, their voice low and distorted.

Mia nodded, her gaze fixed on the figure. "Yes. We're here to find out what you know."

The figure handed Mia a small envelope. "Inside is information about the mole and the next steps of the operation. But be careful. There are others who are watching."

Without another word, the figure turned and disappeared into the darkness. Mia and Jenna opened the envelope, their eyes scanning the contents. The information inside was detailed, revealing potential suspects within the department and suggesting further actions they could take.

As they reviewed the information, a cold wind swept through the docks, adding to the sense of unease. Mia and Jenna knew that the stakes had never been higher, and the danger was far from over. The shadows of betrayal and deception loomed large, and they were determined to uncover the truth and ensure that justice was served.

10

The Fractured Trust

The first light of dawn barely touched the edges of the horizon, casting a pale glow over the city as Mia and Jenna returned to Jenna's apartment from the docks. They were on edge, the gravity of the informant's revelations weighing heavily on them. With the new information in hand, they knew they had to act swiftly but cautiously. The sense of being hunted hung over them, and every sound seemed amplified in the quiet morning hours.

Inside Jenna's apartment, Mia spread out the contents of the envelope on the dining table—a collection of documents detailing potential suspects within the department and a map indicating several locations. The suspicion of a mole had taken their investigation into even more dangerous territory. They needed to act carefully to avoid jeopardizing their progress.

Jenna poured two cups of coffee, her hands steady despite the nervousness etched on her face. "What do you think? Can we trust this information?"

Mia sipped her coffee, her mind racing. "It's hard to say. The informant could be genuine or trying to mislead us. But we need to follow up on it. There's too much at stake to ignore."

The documents included names, department roles, and patterns of suspicious activity that could indicate who the mole might be. The map had several marked locations, each of which could potentially hold crucial information or evidence. Mia and Jenna studied them, trying to discern any connections.

"We need to cross-check this information," Mia said. "Find out if any of these suspects have been involved in recent activities or have had access to sensitive details."

Jenna nodded, her expression resolute. "I'll start on that. Meanwhile, we should decide which location to investigate first."

They decided to focus on a location marked on the map that appeared to be an old warehouse near the edge of the city. It was a spot that hadn't been on their radar before, but the informant's details made it seem worth investigating. As they prepared to leave, the tension between them was palpable. The weight of their mission pressed down heavily, and every decision felt critical.

They arrived at the warehouse, its once bright paint now faded and peeling. The area was desolate, with no signs of recent activity. Mia and Jenna approached cautiously, their senses heightened. The warehouse loomed ahead, an imposing structure that seemed to whisper secrets in the wind.

As they approached, Mia noticed something odd—footprints leading to a side entrance that looked less secure than the main door. "Let's check this side entrance," she suggested.

They moved quietly, their footsteps barely audible on the cracked pavement. The side entrance was slightly ajar, and they pushed it open slowly. The interior of the warehouse was dimly lit by shafts of sunlight streaming through broken windows. Dust particles danced in the beams of light, adding to the eerie atmosphere.

They carefully made their way inside, their eyes scanning the surroundings. The warehouse was filled with old equipment, crates, and machinery. It was clear that it had been unused for some time, but Mia couldn't shake the feeling that they weren't alone.

"Keep your eyes open," Mia whispered. "We don't know what we might find."

They searched the warehouse systematically, moving from one corner to the next. Jenna found a stack of old files hidden behind some crates. She opened one and began to read through it, her eyes widening as she realized it contained records of past transactions and meetings.

"This is exactly what we were looking for," Jenna said, excitement in her voice. "These documents could be evidence of the criminal network's operations."

Mia continued to search the area, her attention focused on a large metal cabinet in the corner. She opened it cautiously, revealing several boxes filled with more documents and a few small electronic devices. She examined the devices, recognizing them as surveillance equipment.

"This confirms that someone has been keeping an eye on things," Mia said. "We need to get this back to the precinct."

Just as they were about to leave, they heard a faint noise coming from the direction of the main entrance. Mia's heart raced. "Someone's coming. We need to hide."

They quickly moved behind a stack of crates, their breaths shallow and controlled. They could hear footsteps growing louder, accompanied by muffled voices. Mia peered around the corner, trying to get a glimpse of who was entering the warehouse.

Three figures emerged into the dim light, their faces obscured by shadows.

They moved with purpose, examining the space as if they were searching for something. Mia and Jenna held their breaths, hoping they wouldn't be discovered.

The figures stopped near the spot where Jenna had found the files. They were clearly professionals, their movements precise and efficient. Mia's heart pounded as she realized that these individuals were likely part of the criminal network they had been investigating.

One of the figures pulled out a small device and began to scan the area. Mia could see that it was a high-tech security tool, possibly used for detecting hidden surveillance equipment. The situation was becoming increasingly dangerous.

Suddenly, Jenna's foot slipped slightly, making a soft noise. One of the figures turned sharply toward their hiding spot. Mia's heart raced as she tensed, preparing for the worst.

The figure's gaze swept the area, and for a moment, it seemed like they had been discovered. But then, the figure turned back to the others, their suspicion apparently not aroused.

Mia and Jenna remained still, their eyes locked on the figures as they continued their search. Minutes passed, feeling like hours. Eventually, the figures moved toward the exit, leaving the warehouse as quietly as they had arrived.

As the warehouse fell silent once more, Mia and Jenna emerged from their hiding spot, their bodies trembling with the aftermath of their close call. They quickly gathered the documents and equipment, making their way out of the warehouse with renewed urgency.

Back in Jenna's apartment, they reviewed the documents they had found. The records detailed various transactions and meetings, providing a clearer picture of the criminal network's operations. The surveillance equipment further confirmed that someone had been monitoring their activities.

The weight of their discovery was overwhelming. The criminal network was more extensive and dangerous than they had imagined, and the mole within the department posed an additional threat. Mia and Jenna knew they needed to act quickly to expose the mole and dismantle the network.

As they prepared to meet with Detective Harris, their resolve hardened. The stakes were higher than ever, and the path ahead was fraught with danger. But they were determined to see the investigation through to the end and ensure that justice was served.

The fractured trust between them and the authorities added to the sense of urgency. They needed to navigate the treacherous waters of betrayal and deceit to uncover the truth and protect themselves from the threats that lurked in the shadows.

11

Undercover Shadows

The night had fallen, draping the city in a cloak of darkness and shrouding it with an eerie quiet. Mia and Jenna, after hours of poring over the evidence they had gathered, were now heading to a covert meeting with Detective Harris. They were both on edge, their nerves taut with anticipation and worry. The newly discovered information had unveiled a deeper layer to the criminal network, and the reality of the mole in their midst cast a long shadow over their mission.

The drive to the secure location was tense. Jenna's grip on the steering wheel was tight, her knuckles white under the streetlights. Mia stared out of the window, her mind racing through scenarios, each one more dangerous than the last. The city's lights flickered past them, and the feeling of being watched seemed almost palpable.

When they arrived at the meeting point—a nondescript building used as a safe house—they found Detective Harris waiting for them in the dimly lit lobby. His expression was grave, and he gestured for them to follow him into a small conference room at the back.

Inside, the room was stark and functional, with only a table, a few chairs, and a whiteboard covered in scribbled notes and sketches. Harris looked up from the whiteboard, his face lined with worry. "We've had a major development," he said, his tone serious.

Mia and Jenna exchanged anxious glances. "What's going on?" Mia asked.

Harris took a deep breath. "We've confirmed that there's indeed a mole within our department. The anonymous tip we received was accurate. We've identified a few suspects, but we can't make any moves until we're absolutely certain."

Jenna's eyes widened. "How did this happen? And what do we do now?"

Harris's gaze was steady. "The mole has been feeding information to the criminal network. We've traced some of the communications, and it's clear that they're aware of our operations. We need to proceed very carefully to avoid alerting them."

He handed them a new set of documents—profiles of the suspected mole and recent communications that hinted at upcoming transactions. The details were alarming, and Mia's mind raced as she tried to piece everything together.

"We have a lead on a major deal happening tomorrow night," Harris continued. "We believe it's going to be a pivotal moment for the criminal network. If we can intercept it, we might be able to catch the mole in the act."

Mia and Jenna nodded, their determination solidifying. "What's the plan?" Mia asked.

"We're going to go undercover," Harris said. "We need to infiltrate the operation and gather as much information as possible. I'll provide you with the necessary cover identities and equipment. But remember, this is extremely dangerous. We're dealing with a network that's already proven to be ruthless."

Jenna's voice was steady. "We understand. We'll do whatever it takes."

Harris handed them a folder containing their cover identities—false names, backgrounds, and documentation that would allow them to blend into the criminal world. He also provided them with communication devices and surveillance equipment for their operation.

The plan was to pose as intermediaries looking to broker a deal with the criminal network. They were to attend a meeting at a warehouse where the transaction was scheduled to take place. It was a risky move, but it was their best chance to gather crucial information and potentially expose the mole.

As the sun set, Mia and Jenna transformed into their undercover personas. Mia became "Clara Adams," a supposed intermediary with connections to various suppliers, while Jenna assumed the role of "Emily Foster," her business associate. They dressed the part—sharp suits, confident demeanor, and the right mix of professionalism and subtle aggression to blend into the criminal world.

They arrived at the warehouse well before the scheduled meeting time. The building was large, with high ceilings and a vast open space that could easily accommodate a significant transaction. The area around it was desolate, with only the occasional stray cat or distant car passing by.

As they approached the entrance, Mia and Jenna's hearts raced. The weight of their mission hung heavily on their shoulders. They exchanged a final glance, their expressions resolute.

Inside, the warehouse was dimly lit, with a few scattered crates and a large table set up for the meeting. A group of men, their faces concealed by hats and scarves, were already there, speaking in low, urgent tones. Mia and Jenna took their places at the table, trying to appear as unthreatening as possible.

Minutes passed, and the atmosphere grew more charged. The men's conversation became more animated as they discussed details of the deal. Mia and Jenna listened intently, their eyes and ears open for any valuable information.

The door to the warehouse creaked open, and a new group of figures entered, their presence commanding immediate attention. Among them was a tall, imposing figure who seemed to be the leader. His gaze swept over the room, and Mia's heart skipped a beat as she recognized him from their previous investigations.

"This is our contact," one of the men said, introducing Mia and Jenna to the leader. "They're here to finalize the deal."

The leader nodded, his eyes cold and calculating. "Let's get down to business," he said, his voice low and authoritative.

The meeting proceeded with tense negotiations, the details of the deal being hashed out with precision and secrecy. Mia and Jenna kept their composure, carefully observing the interactions and jotting down notes. The stakes were high, and any misstep could blow their cover.

Suddenly, Mia noticed a familiar face among the new arrivals—one of the suspects they had identified as a potential mole. The mole's presence confirmed that the meeting was critical and that the risk of exposure was greater than ever.

The negotiations continued, and the atmosphere grew more intense. The leader's demands were steep, and the negotiations reached a critical point. Mia could sense that the deal was about to be closed, and they needed to act quickly to gather the necessary evidence.

Just as the meeting was about to conclude, Jenna subtly activated the surveillance equipment, capturing crucial footage of the interactions and the details of the deal. Mia's heart raced as she tried to remain focused, aware that any sudden move could draw unwanted attention.

The meeting finally wrapped up, and the participants began to disperse. Mia and Jenna managed to slip away unnoticed, their hearts pounding with the adrenaline of their narrow escape. They gathered their equipment and made their way back to their safe house, eager to review the footage and assess their findings.

Back at the safe house, they reviewed the captured footage, their eyes scanning for any significant details. The evidence was revealing—details about the deal, the mole's involvement, and the next steps for the criminal network. It was clear that they had gathered valuable information, but the danger was far from over.

As they prepared to report their findings to Detective Harris, Mia and Jenna knew that their mission was reaching a critical juncture. The mole's involvement was now undeniable, and the criminal network was more dangerous than they had ever imagined.

Their trust in the system was shattered, and the shadow of betrayal loomed large. But they were determined to see the investigation through to its conclusion, no matter the cost. The stakes were higher than ever, and their resolve was unwavering as they prepared for the next phase of their dangerous journey.

12

The Final Gambit

The safe house was a hive of activity, its sparse furnishings and cold, sterile atmosphere starkly contrasting the danger that had become a part of Mia and Jenna's daily lives. The captured footage from the warehouse meeting had provided a wealth of information, but it was clear that their work was far from over. The stakes had never been higher, and with the mole's identity now partially revealed, the need to act swiftly and decisively was paramount.

As the first light of dawn filtered through the thin curtains, Mia and Jenna were already hard at work, poring over the evidence and preparing their next move. Detective Harris had instructed them to stay put and keep a low profile until he could arrange a strategy meeting with the higher-ups. However, the tension was palpable; every passing minute felt like a threat.

The footage revealed a planned exchange of critical information and resources between the criminal network and a foreign buyer, scheduled to take place that evening. The mole's involvement was evident, but the specifics of their role remained unclear. The sense of urgency was overwhelming. The criminal network was on high alert, and the mole's actions were making their every move increasingly perilous.

"Everything is in place for tonight," Jenna said, her voice steady despite the gravity of their situation. "The meeting at the docks will be crucial. We need to make sure we're ready."

Mia nodded, her eyes scanning through the documents. "We've got the details of the transaction, but we still need to figure out how to catch the mole in the act. If we can get concrete evidence, we'll have a better chance of bringing them down."

They decided to head to the docks early to ensure they had ample time to prepare. The location was a large, dilapidated warehouse on the outskirts of town—a perfect setting for covert transactions and clandestine meetings. The area was remote, adding an extra layer of danger but also providing an opportunity for a strategic vantage point.

As they drove to the docks, the cityscape blurred by, the familiar streets now tinged with a sense of foreboding. The plan was to set up surveillance equipment and blend in with the surroundings, observing the transaction from a concealed location. The warehouse was scheduled to be buzzing with activity, and they needed to avoid drawing attention to themselves.

Upon arrival, Mia and Jenna navigated the maze of rusting containers and abandoned machinery to find a suitable vantage point. They chose a small, hidden alcove overlooking the main warehouse area, from which they could monitor the proceedings without being seen. The surveillance equipment was set up with practiced efficiency, and the two women took their positions, their nerves taut with anticipation.

As the evening approached, the atmosphere around the warehouse grew charged with an almost palpable tension. The sounds of distant machinery and the occasional hum of traffic were the only interruptions to the stillness. Mia and Jenna scanned the area, their eyes sharp for any signs of the impending transaction.

At precisely the time indicated in the footage, a convoy of black SUVs arrived at the warehouse, their engines rumbling loudly in the otherwise quiet night. The vehicles were heavily guarded, and the sight of them sent a chill down Mia's spine. This was it—the culmination of their efforts, and potentially, the breaking point of their mission.

The warehouse doors creaked open, and the figures began to emerge. Men in dark suits and masks, their faces hidden, began unloading crates and boxes. Mia's heart raced as she recognized some of the individuals from the earlier footage. The atmosphere was tense, every movement and gesture observed with critical attention.

As the activity inside the warehouse intensified, Mia and Jenna noticed a new arrival—a figure who moved with an air of authority and confidence. Their face was obscured, but Mia could sense the importance of this individual. They were likely a key player in the transaction and possibly the mole.

The transaction began, and the men exchanged briefcases filled with cash for crates of contraband. Mia adjusted the surveillance equipment, capturing every moment of the exchange. The stakes were incredibly high; they needed to ensure that every detail was recorded and that they could make their presence known if necessary.

Suddenly, a loud crash echoed through the warehouse. Mia and Jenna froze, their hearts pounding. The noise came from the direction of the main doors, and it was clear that something had gone wrong. The men inside the warehouse began to move with increased urgency, their voices rising in alarm.

Mia glanced at Jenna, her expression tense. "We need to find out what's happening. This could be our chance to catch the mole."

They cautiously made their way closer to the warehouse, moving stealthily to avoid detection. As they approached, they saw that the commotion was caused by a group of men who had burst in, weapons drawn. It was clear that an unplanned confrontation had erupted.

In the chaos, Mia spotted the mole among the commotion. The mole was trying to blend in with the other figures, but their anxious demeanor and hurried movements made them stand out. Mia's heart pounded as she realized that this was the moment they had been waiting for.

Jenna signaled for Mia to follow her as they maneuvered through the shadows, carefully positioning themselves to get a clearer view. The situation was rapidly deteriorating, and the potential for violence was escalating. The confrontation between the different factions grew more intense, and it was becoming increasingly difficult to keep track of the mole's actions.

Mia could see the mole talking to one of the armed men, their conversation intense and urgent. It was clear that the mole was trying to negotiate or perhaps make a desperate attempt to salvage the situation. The stakes were incredibly high, and Mia knew they had to act quickly.

Suddenly, the sounds of sirens began to wail in the distance. The approaching law enforcement created a new layer of urgency. The warehouse became a frenzy of activity, with figures scrambling to escape. Mia and Jenna used the confusion to their advantage, moving quickly to capture the mole on camera.

In the chaos, Mia managed to get a clear shot of the mole's face as they attempted to flee. The identification was crucial; it would be the key to linking the mole to the criminal network and bringing them to justice.

As the scene unfolded, law enforcement arrived at the warehouse, surrounding the building and moving in to apprehend the suspects. The confrontation was swift and decisive, with officers securing the area and taking control of the situation.

Mia and Jenna watched from their hidden vantage point, their breaths held in anticipation. The culmination of their efforts was unfolding before them, and they knew that their actions would have significant repercussions.

As the dust began to settle and the warehouse was secured, Mia and Jenna made their way back to their safe house. They were exhausted but exhilarated, knowing that they had played a crucial role in a major operation. The evidence they had gathered, along with the identification of the mole, would be instrumental in dismantling the criminal network and ensuring that justice was served.

Their journey had been fraught with danger and uncertainty, but they had navigated the treacherous waters with determination and skill. As they prepared to debrief with Detective Harris and provide their findings, Mia and Jenna knew that their mission was coming to a close. The final gambit had been played, and the outcome of their efforts would have a profound impact on the fight against crime and corruption.